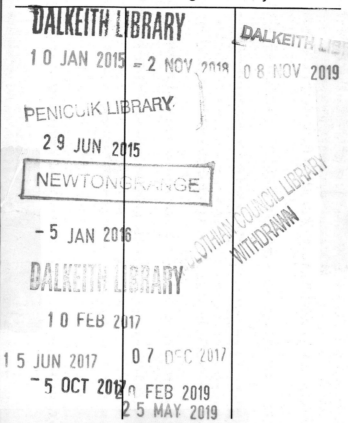

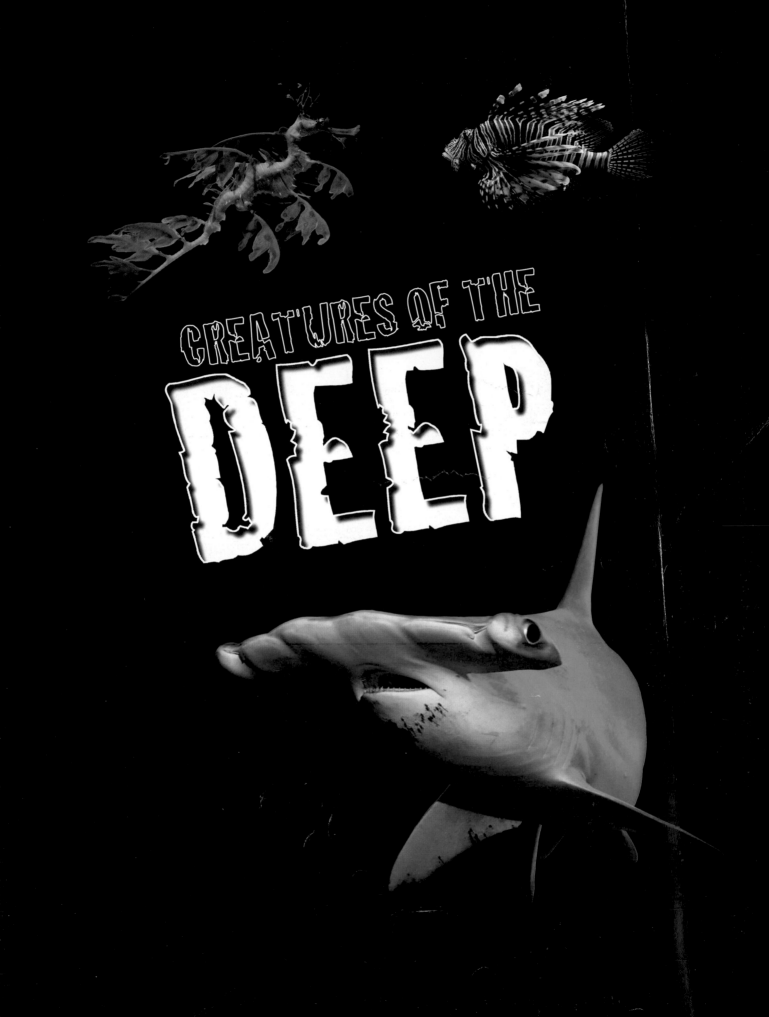

CREATURES OF THE
DEEP

Written by Camilla de la Bédoyère

Editors: Emma Marriot and Jon Richards

Designers: Malcolm Parchment, Marissa Renzullo, and Siân Willams

Art Director: Susi Martin

Publisher: Zeta Jones

CREATURES OF THE
DEEP

CAMILLA DE LA BÉDOYÈRE

QED

QED Publishing

CONTENTS

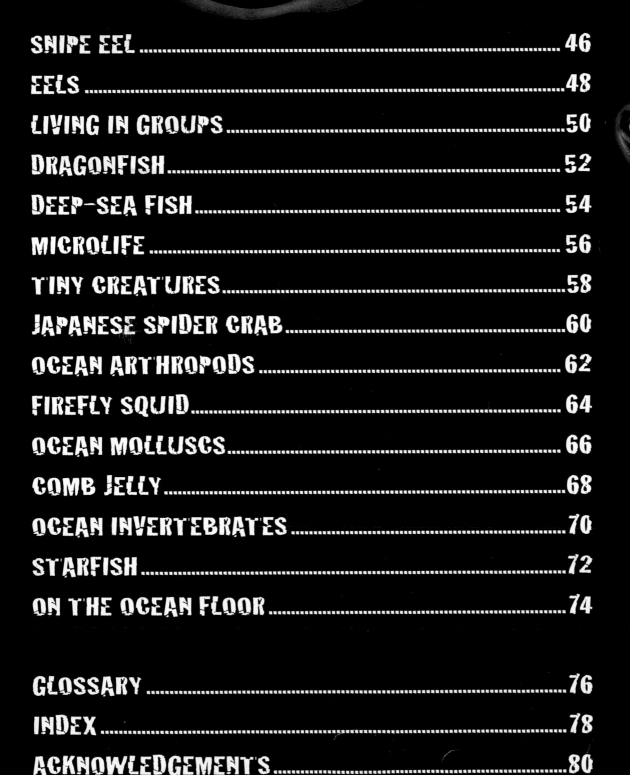

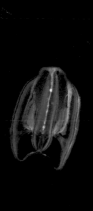

LIFE AT SEA

Plankton
up to 100 m

**Japanese
spider crab**
up to 600 m

Our oceans and seas are home to many animals – from creatures that are too small to see to the world's biggest animal. We have found tens of thousands of species of ocean animals, but there may thousands more waiting to be discovered.

A squid swims through sunlit waters in the Photic Zone.

GIANTS OF THE DEEP

The largest animal that has ever lived on Earth is the blue whale. Even a baby blue whale weighs more than an elephant! Ocean animals can grow big, because the water supports their bulky bodies, allowing them to move and feed freely and without being crushed by their own mass.

PHOTIC ZONE

Sunlight passes through the Photic Zone, which descends to about 200 metres. However, the water quickly absorbs different colours of light the lower you go, including red, yellow and orange light. Only blue light is able to reach the lowest parts of the Photic Zone. Below this is the Aphotic Zone, which is completely dark.

Submersibles *are built to survive the huge pressures deep beneath the surface.*

Blue whale
up to 200 m

Sail fish
up to 200 m

Weddell seal
up to 740 m

Firefly squid
up to 400 m

PHOTIC

Hatchetfish
up to 1000 m

Leatherback turtle
up to 1200 m

1000 M

Great white shark
up to 1900 m

Snipe eel
up to 1800 m

Dragonfish
up to 1800 m

2000 M

Deep-sea angler
up to 2000 m

Sperm whale
up to 3000 m

APHOTIC

Ratfish
up to 3000 m

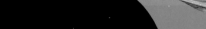

3000 M

SUBMERSIBLE

Submersibles are vessels that
travel deep underwater.
Scientists use them to find out
more about the ocean and the
animals that live in it. These
underwater craft are fitted with
powerful lights to see in the inky
darkness, and robotic arms to
collect sample specimens.

Flashlight fish
up to 4000 m

Starfish
up to 6000 m

4000 M

Comb jelly
up to 7000 m

BLUE WHALE

The mighty blue whale makes massive journeys across the world's oceans, in search of food and a safe place to reproduce. This is the largest animal alive today – and probably the largest animal that has ever lived on Earth.

Blubber
Underneath the whale's skin is a thick layer of blubber – this is fat which the whale uses for energy.

BLUE WHALE
BALAENOPTERA MUSCULUS

DEPTH
0 m

200 m

SIZE • 25–32 M

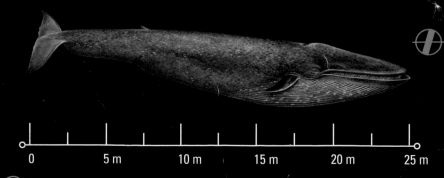

0   5 m   10 m   15 m   20 m   25 m

✛ THROAT GROOVES

When a blue whale gulps in water to filter out tiny krill, grooves allow the whale to expand its throat up to five times its normal size.

The flukes are the large horizontal parts of a whale's tail.

FLUKE

When a blue whale dives it does a 'headstand'. Its tail, which has huge horizontal flukes, rises above the water, and pushes the animal down to depths of nearly 200 m.

Small dorsal fin

Long, narrow fins
A blue whale uses them to change direction as it swims.

On the surface, *whales blow out a plume of water while breathing.*

 GIANT OF THE DEEP

Blue whales are about 26 m long and weigh up to 120 tonnes. That's the same weight as 24 elephants! Their hearts are the size of a small car and their tongues are bigger than a hippopotamus. To fuel this huge mass, an adult blue whale will eat about 3.5 tonnes of krill every day.

BLOWHOLES

Blue whales breathe in air, not water. They have two blowholes on the top of their heads, which they use to breathe when they surface.

BALEEN WHALES

Most baleen whales are huge, but they feed on tiny sea animals. Blue whales, grey whales and humpbacks are all baleen whales. They have special feeding structures in their mouths which they use to capture small animals, but they need to eat billions of them to survive.

Markings
These white patches are different on every animal.

HUMPBACK WHALES

Humpbacks are clever animals that often live in family groups, called pods. They are also acrobatic, despite weighing as much as 400 men, and often leap out of the water in powerful breaching displays.

An Antarctic dwarf minke spy hops above ice floes in the Southern Ocean.

SPY HOPPING

A whale will sometimes pop its head above the water to look around. This action is called spy hopping and some whales hold this position for a minute or more.

Long body
The body of a humpback whale is up to 14 m long.

Long fins
The fins are knobbly and up to one-third of the total body length.

Baleen bristles

BARNACLES
These small animals, called barnacles, have settled on a grey whale's skin. There may be thousands of them weighing 150 kg on just one whale.

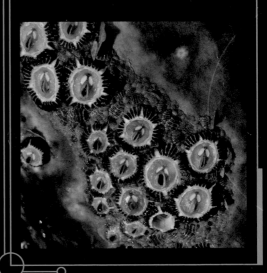

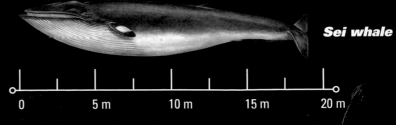

Sei whale

0   5 m   10 m   15 m   20 m

BALEEN PLATE
The special structures that these whales use to trap food are called baleen plates. They hang from the roof of a whale's mouth and work like sieves to capture small animals when the whale gulps in a mouthful of water. They are made of nail-like protein, and bristles line the inside layers.

SEI WHALES
These large baleen whales are found in most of the world's oceans. They grow to nearly 20 m long and can weigh nearly 30 tonnes.

SPERM WHALE

Sperm whales are one of world's largest predators. They can dive deeper than any other mammal, swimming to the cold, dark depths of an ocean in search of prey, such as octopus or the enormous giant squid.

SPERM WHALE
PHYSETER MACROCEPHALUS

DEPTH

0 m

3000 m

SIZE • UP TO 20.5 M

Large head
Sperm whales have the largest brains in the animal world.

Battle scars
Many sperm whales have scars from battles with giant squid.

 ## LIGHT HEADED

A sperm whale has a waxy substance in its head called spermaceti. It may help the whale float, but the whale might also use spermaceti to make sounds.

A mother and calf sperm whale swimming close to the ocean surface.

WHALE DIVING

During its hunt for prey, a sperm whale can dive to 3,000 metres, and stay underwater for two hours.

A sperm whale diving head-first into the deep.

MOTHER AND CALF

A baby whale is called a calf. A sperm whale calf feeds on its mother's milk for 13 years! Sperm whales may attack boats if they think their young are in danger.

Huge, heavy body
A male sperm whale is three times heavier than a female. Each whale needs to eat about 1 tonne of food a day!

SKULL

Sperm whales are toothed whales. They have up to 100 teeth on the lower jaw, but no teeth on the upper jaw.

Sharp teeth

TOOTHED WHALES

There are about 85 species of whale, and most of them are toothed whales. These mammals hunt for fish or other sea creatures and most of them are intelligent animals that live in family groups. Dolphins and porpoises are small toothed whales.

A lucky seal runs away from a charging killer whale as it beaches itself.

Stout body
A thick layer of blubber under a beluga's skin keeps it warm.

KILLER WHALE
Killer whales are also called orcas. They are deadly hunters that can swim onto the land to grab seals to eat.

NARWHAL
A narwhal's long 'horn' is actually a tooth, or 'tusk'. No one knows exactly why narwhals grow such long tusks.

Long tusk

BELUGA WHALES

Beluga whales are small toothed whales that live in cold Arctic waters. They are sociable and communicate with clicking sounds. They can even copy noises made by other animals.

Melon
The rounded forehead of a toothed whale is called a melon.

Dolphin skull
Bottlenose dolphins have a large beak-like mouth with about 50 cone-shaped teeth.

DOLPHINS

Dolphins often gather in groups, called pods. Atlantic spotted dolphins hunt for fish and crabs hiding on the sea floor.

These spotted dolphins will live, hunt and breed together in a pod.

Wide mouth
Beluga whales are popular with divers, because they seem to smile!

WHITE WHALES

Male beluga whales can grow up to 5.5 m long and weigh 1.5 tonnes. Its white body is perfect camouflage against the ice and it has no dorsal fin on its back.

WEDDELL SEAL

Weddell seals are plump seals with a thick layer of fat, or blubber, to keep them warm. They are able to survive in the icy Antarctic, which is the coldest place on Earth. Weddell seals hunt fish in the Southern Ocean, which surrounds Antarctica.

Tube body
A seal's body is the perfect shape for moving quickly through water.

Grey fur
Seals are mammals and they have a short, thick coat of hair to keep them warm.

FACT FILE

DIET
Fish, crustaceans, octopuses

HABITAT
Coastal waters around Antarctica

FEEDING TIME

An active adult Weddell seal will eat about 50 kg of food in a day. If the water is dark or cloudy, they will track prey using their sensitive whiskers.

SUPERB SWIMMERS

These animals are superb swimmers and dive below thick layers of ice. They can stay underwater for 45 minutes at a time, foraging for food or trying to find new breathing holes.

A mother and pup pop their heads above the ice to breathe.

BREATHING HOLES

Weddell seals breathe air. They make holes in the ice so that they can surface and breathe between dives.

WEDDELL SEAL
LEPTONYCHOTES WEDDELLII

DEPTH

0 m

740 m

SIZE • UP TO 3 M

The forward-facing eyes give a Weddell seal 3-D vision, which is vital for hunting.

UNDERWATER

Weddell seals are hunters. They use their big, forward-facing eyes to find fish, even in the dimly lit waters of a polar ocean.

For the first few weeks, a baby seal is helpless and relies on its mother completely.

Flippers
Seals have two pairs of flippers. The hind pair stops the seal from rolling in the water as it swims.

SEAL PUPS

Baby seals are called pups. Females give birth on the Antarctic ice, and the pups cannot swim until they are one to two weeks old.

SEALS AND SEA LIONS

Seals and sea lions are animals that live both on land and in the water. They belong to a group of swimming mammals called pinnipeds. Seals and sea lions are similar, but sea lions have ear flaps and longer, hairless front flippers which they use to 'fly' through the water.

Flippers
By flapping their flippers, seals and sea lions can move through the water very quickly.

STELLER'S SEA LION
Steller's sea lions are large predators that chase squid, octopuses, fish and even other seals in the Pacific Ocean.

Steller's sea lions are hunted by killer whales and white sharks.

CAPE FUR SEAL
Cape fur seals can twist and turn in the water, changing direction at speed when they are chasing a shoal of fish.

Harp seal pups are covered in thick white fur.

HARP SEAL PUP
Harp seals are found in the Arctic. They can live to be 35 years old and they mostly hunt fish, such as cod.

An enormous male walrus resting on an ice floe.

WALRUS

Walruses are huge pinnipeds with enormous teeth, or tusks. They use their tusks to fight each other, break holes in the ice and to pull themselves out of the water.

Ear
There is no ear flap on this seal's head.

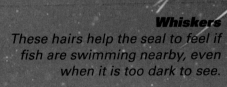

Whiskers
These hairs help the seal to feel if fish are swimming nearby, even when it is too dark to see.

CLUMSY WALKERS

On land, the fins and flippers of seals and sea lions make them slow, clumsy walkers. However, unlike other marine mammals, such as whales and dolphins, seals and sea lions have to come on to dry land in order to give birth.

LEATHERBACK TURTLE

Leatherback turtles are the biggest of all the turtles that live in the sea. They breathe air, but they can dive deep in search of their favourite prey, jellyfish. They hold their breath for more than 30 minutes at a time.

A leatherback turtle will lay about 80 eggs in one go.

LAYING EGGS

Females use their flippers to dig a burrow in soft sand, and lay her eggs in it.

Once they have hatched, baby turtles have to race to the sea unprotected from waiting predators.

HATCHLINGS

When the hatchlings break out of their eggs they must find their way to the sea before any predator can catch them.

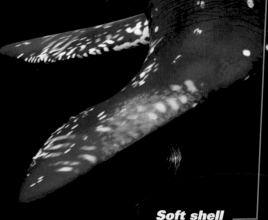

SPINES

The backward-pointing spines in a leatherback's mouth and throat stop slippery jellyfish from slipping back out of the turtle's mouth.

Soft shell
Most turtles and tortoises have a hard shell, but the shell of this turtle is like leather.

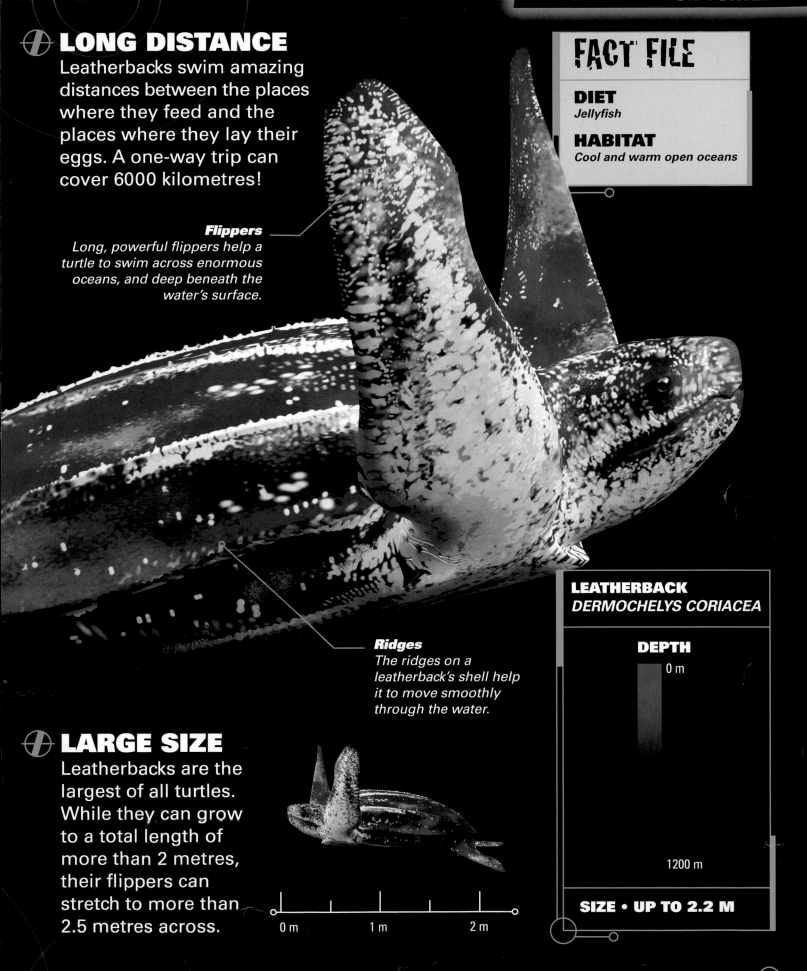

LONG DISTANCE

Leatherbacks swim amazing distances between the places where they feed and the places where they lay their eggs. A one-way trip can cover 6000 kilometres!

Flippers
Long, powerful flippers help a turtle to swim across enormous oceans, and deep beneath the water's surface.

FACT FILE

DIET
Jellyfish

HABITAT
Cool and warm open oceans

Ridges
The ridges on a leatherback's shell help it to move smoothly through the water.

LARGE SIZE

Leatherbacks are the largest of all turtles. While they can grow to a total length of more than 2 metres, their flippers can stretch to more than 2.5 metres across.

0 m   1 m   2 m

LEATHERBACK
DERMOCHELYS CORIACEA

DEPTH
0 m

1200 m

SIZE • UP TO 2.2 M

OCEAN REPTILES

Most reptiles live on land, but some types have taken to a life at sea. Like all reptiles, they lay their eggs on land, although some sea snakes give birth to their young in water. Marine reptiles are more common in warm oceans than cool ones.

BANDED SEA KRAIT

The bright stripes of banded sea kraits act as a warning and show that they are venomous sea snakes. They return to the land to mate and lay eggs.

Banded sea krait

BEAKED SEA SNAKE

Beaked sea snakes are one of the deadliest of all snakes, with powerful venom that can kill a human quickly.

Feet
The clawed feet are webbed, so a crocodile can swim quickly through the water.

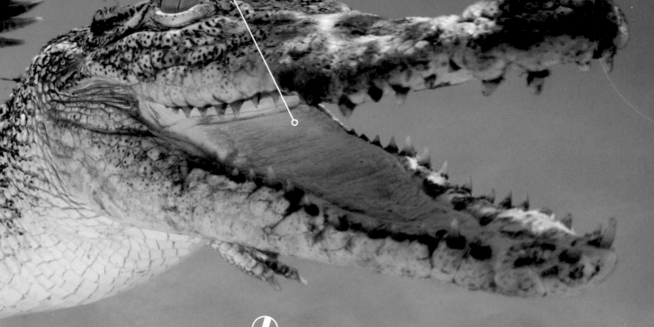

Snout
Crocodiles can open their mouths underwater because a special flap at the back of their throat closes to stop water rushing in.

Nostrils
A crocodile's nostrils are at the tip of its long snout. It can breathe out underwater, but must return to the surface to breathe in.

SALTWATER CROCODILE

Crocodiles can grow huge, but saltwater crocodiles – or 'salties' – are the monsters of the family. They may grow to 7 metres long, and can live in rivers or the sea.

GREEN TURTLE

Green turtles feed on plants that grow in the sea. Like most sea turtles they are at risk of becoming extinct.

The olive sea snake can close its nostrils when underwater.

OLIVE SEA SNAKE

An olive sea snake's nostrils are on the top of its head, so it can breathe at the sea's surface. Unlike land snakes, it also has a flattened rear section to its tail, which is ideal for swimming.

Green turtle

GREAT WHITE SHARK

Fin
The large fin on the back, called the dorsal fin, is the shape of a triangle.

A lean, mean powerful hunter with razor-sharp teeth – this is one of the world's most impressive predators. Few animals inspire as much fear as a great white shark, but these big beasts rarely eat humans.

A great white breaches with a helpless seal in its mouth.

BREACHING
Great whites can leap out of the water to catch their prey. This is called breaching.

SENSITIVE HUNTER
Great white sharks are ambush hunters. They can sense prey from far away. They can then accelerate to speeds of more than 55 km/h to catch an animal – before crunching down on it with their massive jaws.

FACT FILE

DIET
Large animals such as seals, tuna, sharks, sea birds and turtles

HABITAT
The open ocean and coasts, especially shallow water

0	2 m	4 m	6 m

GREAT WHITE SHARK
CARCHARODON

DEPTH

0 m

1900 m

SIZE • UP TO 6 M

Gill slits
There are five large gill slits on each side of the head.

Powerful tail
Packed with muscles, the shark moves this from side to side to push itself through the water.

TEETH
A great white has about 30 teeth in a row on each jaw, but there are another four rows of teeth behind those. As one falls out, another moves forwards to take its place.

Serrated teeth
The edges of the teeth are serrated (jagged) so that they can slice through prey easily.

Great whites are one of the few sharks that spy hop.

Hunting fish
Great white sharks are the largest predatory fish on the planet. They can weigh more than 2 tonnes.

SHARKS

Sharks are fish that hunt other animals to eat. They have rough skin and soft skeletons, like skates and rays. There are about 400 different types of shark, from small ones that live near the seabed to large hunters of the open ocean.

⊕ WHALE SHARK

Whale sharks are not just the largest sharks, they are the largest fish in the world. They may be big, but whale sharks are harmless to humans and only eat small animals, such as plankton.

HAMMERHEAD SHARK

Hammerhead sharks have strangely shaped heads. This head shape may help a hammerhead to find its prey, and change direction quickly.

Spotted skin
Every whale shark has a different pattern on its back.

Wide mouth
The mouth measures about 2 metres across, but the teeth are tiny.

A sand tiger shark usually swims with its mouth open, showing the rows of jagged teeth.

SHARK SKIN

Sharks do not have scales. Their skin is covered in tiny 'teeth' instead. They contain a hard substance called enamel, just like our teeth.

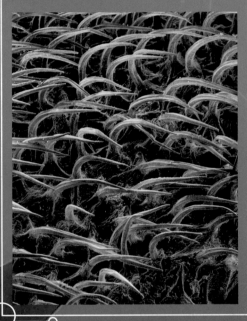

SAND TIGERS

Sand tiger sharks are often called 'raggedtooths'. Their long, pointy teeth are perfect for gripping hold of slippery fish and squid.

Huge body
Most whale sharks can grow up to 11 metres long.

SEA GIANT

A whale shark can weigh in at more than 20 tonnes – that's the weight of four elephants. It is one of only three species of filter-feeding shark, the other two being the basking shark and the very rare megamouth.

Friendly fish
Smaller fish often swim near whale sharks, hiding from animals that might want to eat them!

MIGRATIONS

Many animals go on long journeys to find food or mates. These journeys are called migrations, and some of the world's greatest migrations happen in the oceans. All sorts of animals migrate, from giant blue whales to tiny krill.

Ball of fish
Thousands of sardines gather together to make a baitball to try and stay safe from predators.

BLUE WHALE
Blue whales spend the summer in the cold waters of the Arctic or Antarctic, where they feed. They then swim thousands of kilometres to breed in warm waters during the winter.

BLUE SHARK
Female blue sharks go on an incredible migration of about 16,000 km to breed. These sharks give birth to live young and a litter can contain more than 100 baby sharks.

Large eyes

Large pectoral fins

BALL OF SARDINES

Billions of sardines gather in huge shoals near South Africa in the winter. They are here to feast on tiny plankton. Hungry predators follow the sardines on their migration.

Five pairs of swimming legs

ANTARCTIC KRILL

These tiny animals go on long vertical journeys in the ocean. This means they travel up or down, in the water in search of food.

SOCKEYE SALMON

Sockeye salmon live in the ocean until it is time to spawn (lay eggs). They leave the oceans and swim to lakes or rivers to mate.

The baitball distracts predators

Predators
Large predators, such as seals, sharks and sailfish, come to feast on a baitball.

RATFISH

Ratfish are peculiar fish that are close relatives of sharks, skates and rays. They have stout, flabby bodies, rough skin and no scales. Ratfish normally swim close to the seabed where they find crunchy animals to eat, crushing them with their plate-like teeth.

FACT FILE

DIET
Crustaceans, echinoderms, worms, fish

HABITAT
Near the seafloor in the Northeast Pacific Ocean

Long, slender tail
This animal is called a ratfish because of the shape and size of its tail.

Long fins
Fins run along the length of the whip-like tail.

SPECIAL CLASPERS
Like male sharks, male ratfish have special claspers on their bodies (visible just behind the lower fins). They use them to clasp (hold) onto females at mating time.

Ratfish lay their eggs in sand or mud on the seabed.

RATFISH EGG
Female ratfish lay a single spoon-shaped egg every 10-14 days at breeding time. Each egg is protected inside a rubbery egg case.

RATFISH
HYDROLAGUS COLLIEI

DEPTH

0 m

3000 m

SIZE • 30 CM

Despite its large eyes, most of its prey is found using the fish's sense of smell.

RABBIT FACE
Ratfish have large eyes, broad mouths and strange heads that are often said to look like rabbit heads.

Spotted skin
Spots on the skin help a fish to blend into the sea floor so predators cannot see it.

VENOMOUS FISH
A ratfish has a long spine on its back, just in front of the dorsal fin. This spine is connected to a venom gland. Although the venom is not fatal to humans, it can produce a painful burning sensation that lasts for a couple of days.

RAYS AND CARTILAGE FISH

Most fish have bony skeletons, but there is another large group of fish in the oceans – the cartilaginous fish. These fish have skeletons made of a rubbery material called cartilage, instead of bone. This is the same material that is found in your nose and outer ears. Cartilaginous fish include sharks, ratfish, rays and skates.

Tail
Manta ray tails are usually shorter than their bodies.

Electric ray

Stingray tail

ELECTRIC RAY
There are 14 species, or type, of electric ray. They catch their prey by stunning them with a powerful jolt of electricity.

STINGRAY
Stingrays usually swim near the seabed. They defend themselves using a whip-like tail that has a venomous spine.

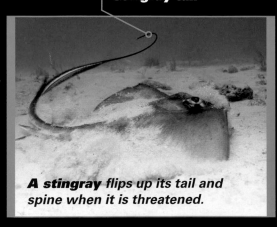

*A **stingray** flips up its tail and spine when it is threatened.*

Fins
A manta ray's huge fins beat like wings, so the fish appears to slowly fly through the water.

Guitarfish take their name from the rounded guitar shape of their heads.

GUITARFISH

Guitarfish live in warm coastal waters, where they prowl above the sea floor looking for crustaceans and prawns to eat.

MANTA RAY

Manta rays are enormous, peaceful fish that feed on plankton and can measure more than 7 metres across. They may be big, but they are graceful fish that can even leap out of the water. Manta rays give birth to their young.

Mouth horns
The large mouth opens to suck in water and tiny living things called plankton. Horn-shaped edges force plankton into the fish's mouth.

EAGLE RAY

Eagle rays are kite-shaped fish that often live in large shoals. They are good swimmers, and have a venomous spine on their tail.

SAILFISH

Sailfish are the fastest swimming fish in the sea. They have huge sail-like fins that help them to reach top speeds of about 70 km/h, and to leap out of the water. Sailfish often hunt in a group and usually swim near the ocean surface.

Microscopic juvenile

JUVENILES
Female sailfish produce about 4 million eggs at a time! The young do not grow their bills until they are about 6 millimetres long.

Large body
A sailfish's body is streamlined, which means it is the right shape for moving quickly through water.

Huge dorsal fin
The fin on a sailfish's back is tall and almost stretches the whole length of the body.

SAILFISH
ISTIOPHORUS PLATYPTERUS

DEPTH

0 m

200 m

SIZE • UP TO 3 M

SUPER SPEED
Sailfish need speed to catch the fast-swimming fish, such as mackerel and sardines, that they prefer. These long-nosed swimmers belong to a family of fish called billfishes.

FACT FILE

DIET
Schooling fish, octopuses and squid

HABITAT
Warm, open oceans

POINTED NOSE
A sailfish's mouth is long and slender. It is called a bill because it looks like the slim bill of a bird.

The bill can measure nearly one-third of the fish's length.

Bill
The fish's upper jaw is about twice as long as its lower jaw.

⊕ ALL CHANGE
Sailfish have the ability to change the colour of their skin. When they become excited, they can create a range of colours, including greys, purples and silvers to confuse prey.

Sailfish sometimes use their large sails to herd prey together.

HUNTING FISH
The fish uses its sword-like bill to slash at shoaling fish. It then swallows any fish that have been injured or stunned.

OTHER BONY FISH

There are about 31,000 species of bony fish and most of them live in the oceans, ranging from tiny dwarf goby to the giant ocean sunfish. Although they have skeletons of bone, these fish come in all shapes and sizes. Some of them hunt other animals to eat, while others eat plants.

PORCUPINE FISH

When a porcupine fish is resting it may look odd, but it does not look too scary. When it fills itself with air, the fish's body turns into a ball of spines that a predator won't try and swallow!

 ## SUNFISH

Sunfish are the largest bony fish in the world. They live in warm waters and swim slowly, nibbling at jellyfish. If a sunfish is scared it might jump out of the water.

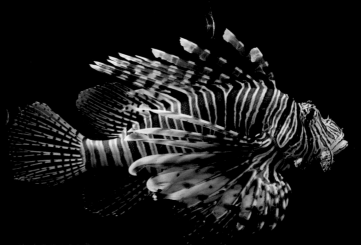

LIONFISH

Lionfish live around coral reefs. Their bold stripes warn other animals that their fins are covered in venomous spines.

Ocean
sunfish
larva

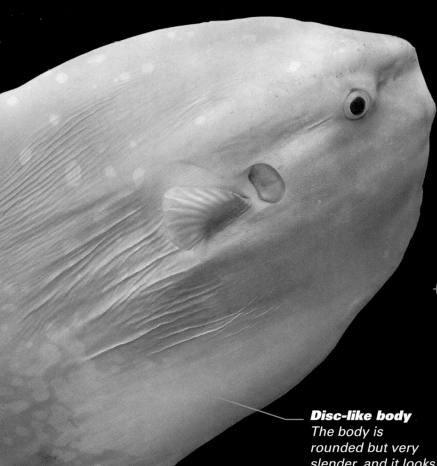

Disc-like body
The body is
rounded but very
slender, and it looks
like a disc, or a sun.

Tails and fins
Sunfish have unusual tails with
a frilled edge. The fins are
shaped like triangles and slice
through the water like blades.

⊕ TINY LARVAE

Sunfish larvae are only
2.5 mm long and will grow
many millions of times in
size before reaching maturity.
Some larvae are also covered
in spines, which they lose as
they grow.

LEAFY SEADRAGON

Leafy seadragons are a type
of seahorse. Their incredible
body shape helps them to
hide in seaweed.

Fins look like seaweed

Hagfish can tie themselves
in knots to escape from predators.

HAGFISH

Hagfish have long eel-like bodies that
are covered in sticky slime. They do not
have jaws, and some scientists think
they are not really fish at all!

DEEP-SEA ANGLERFISH

This terrifying-looking fish has a long thin fin just above its mouth, topped with a light. This fin and light are used like a fishing rod to attract prey, including small fish and squid, which probably mistake the light for a tasty snack.

Small fin
As they don't have to move quickly to catch prey, most anglerfish are slow swimmers.

Stretchy body
An anglerfish can stretch its body to engulf prey twice its size.

DEEP-SEA ANGLERFISH
MELANOCETUS JOHNSONI

DEPTH

200 m

2000 m

SIZE • 20–90 CM

ACTUAL • SIZE

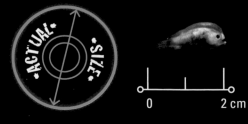

0   2 cm

LITTLE AND LARGE

Female anglerfish are about 20 cm long, while the male (left) can be less than a tenth of this size. Females are the only ones to have lights.

HIDING IN THE DARK

Living at depths of between 200–2000 m, deep-sea anglerfish are coloured dark brown or black. This camouflages them in the coal-black water.

Skeleton
The red areas are the fish's bones.

OPEN WIDE

Its thin, flexible bones, jelly-like skin and stretchy stomach allow the anglerfish to open its mouth wide enough to swallow prey much larger than itself.

Sharp teeth
Its needle-like teeth pierce the flesh of its victims.

MALES AND FEMALES

In some species of anglerfish, the much-smaller males attach themselves to the females, feeding off nutrients in the females' blood.

ANGLERFISH

There are more than 200 species of anglerfish. They come in many shapes and sizes, including the round football fish and the long, thin wonder fish. In some species, the teeth can be pushed back so that they don't stop anything entering the mouth.

Lure
This contains millions of light-making bacteria.

Humpback anglerfish
Females of this anglerfish species can grow up to 20 cm long, and they are found at depths of up to 2000 m.

LITTLE GUY

During mating, the tiny male of most anglerfish species attaches himself to the female. His body then fuses with hers.

Sharp teeth
Backward-facing teeth stop prey from escaping.

OUTER SHELL
Some anglerfish young are covered in a thick protective membrane when they are born.

Short tail

WONDER FISH
Unlike other angler fish, the 9-cm-long wonder fish's lure is inside its mouth.

ALL DEPTHS
Anglerfish range in size from 4–90 cm in length. Some live in shallow waters, but the deepest living are found more than 2 km down. Many are slow swimmers. Some even lie on the ocean bed, mouth open, waiting for prey to come into range.

Like a ball
The fish has a short, sphere-shaped body.

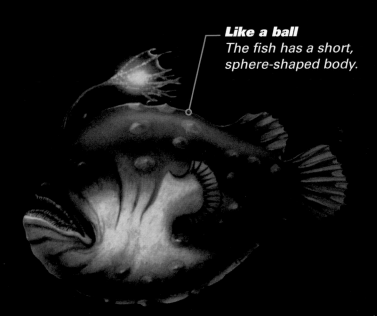

SUDDEN BURSTS
While anglerfish spend most of their time hovering in the water or moving slowly, some have been seen making short bursts of speed to avoid hunters.

FOOTBALL FISH
The first species of angler fish ever discovered, the football fish ranges in size from 4–40 cm and is found at depths between 200–1000 m.

HATCHETFISH

Hatchetfish are creatures of the twilight zone, where there is little light. However, they also swim up towards the lighter zones to feed during the night. About 50 species of hatchetfish have been discovered so far.

Flat, shiny body
This helps to reflect any small amount of light.

FACT FILE

DIET
Fish, plankton and small crustaceans

HABITAT
Deep water in warm areas of the oceans

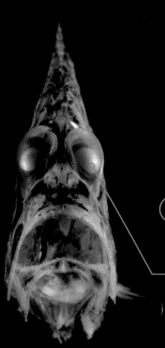

Tube-shaped eyes
They point upwards, towards the light.

ACTUAL · SIZE

BIG EYES
A hatchetfish's strange eyes are fixed looking upwards and are shaped to catch as much light as possible. The fish uses them to look for any prey swimming above.

0   2 cm   4 cm   6 cm

HATCHETFISH
STERNOPTYCHINAE

DEPTH
0 m

1000 m

SIZE · 7.5 CM

LIGHT ORGANS

A hatchetfish has special light-making organs called photophores. These glow to match any light coming from the surface above, hiding the fish from any predators looking up from the depths below.

BELLY LIGHTS

A hatchetfish's photophores are found lining its belly and pointing down into the deep inky blackness.

Axe body
The fish's body is the shape of an axe (or 'hatchet').

Photophores
Light-making organs line the fish's body.

MARINE HATCHETFISH

There are about 40 species of marine hatchetfish. There is another group of freshwater hatchetfish, but they are not related to these sea-living species.

FLASHLIGHT FISH

It may be dark in the deep ocean, but there are fish that can make light to help them find other animals to eat. Flashlight fish usually stay in the darkest parts of the ocean, but will travel to shallow water to feed on small crustaceans at night.

FACT FILE

DIET
Small animals, especially crustaceans

HABITAT
Deep waters in warmer parts of the ocean

Slender body
The body is covered with shiny scales.

Large eyes
Eyes that are big can gather more light than ones that are small.

Photophore
This is the place where light is made. Fish can have photophores on different parts of their bodies.

GLOW IN THE DARK

Like anglerfish, flashlight fish use their lights to lure prey. They also use their lights to communicate, and to confuse animals that want to eat them.

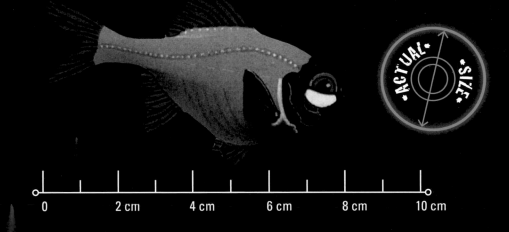

FLASHLIGHT FISH
ANOMALOPIDAE

DEPTH

0 m

4000 m

SIZE • 8 CM

•ACTUAL• •SIZE•

0   2 cm   4 cm   6 cm   8 cm   10 cm

BIOLUMINESCENT LIGHT ORGAN

Fish make light in their light organs when two chemicals are mixed together, or the light is made by bacteria that live on the fish's body. Flashlight fish control how much light is on show by covering the light organs with a special flap.

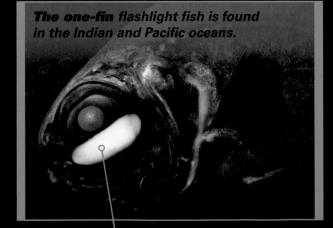

The one-fin flashlight fish is found in the Indian and Pacific oceans.

Photophore covered by flap

Photophore

SNIPE EEL

A snipe eel may look like a long piece of string, but it is a deep-sea fish with a peculiar mouth, big eyes and a very long backbone. It has large eyes to see in the dark ocean waters and its jaws are lined with tiny teeth for catching food.

Long body
Snipe eels have up to 750 bones (vertebrae) in their backbones. That is more than any other animal.

Snipe eel larva

The young have transparent, leaf-shaped bodies.

SNIPE EEL YOUNG

After hatching, a young snipe eel will float near the sea's surface for several months, before sinking to the seabed and changing into an adult.

NIGHT-TIME FEEDERS

Snipe eels probably swim towards the surface of the sea at night, to feed on shrimps and shrimp-like animals. They hang in the water with their mouths open, trapping their prey with backwards-pointing teeth. Once snagged, the prey is then worked into the mouth and swallowed.

FACT FILE

DIET
Shrimp and other crustaceans

HABITAT
Cool and warm oceans

DUCK HEAD

The snipe eel is sometimes called a deep sea duck, because the beak-like mouth makes it look like a duck!

The tips of the snipe eel's long, slender jaws curve apart.

Deep fish
Bobtail snipe eels have been found at depths of 5000 m.

Bobtail snipe eel

BOBTAIL SNIPE EEL

Bobtail snipe eels live in very deep water and they are almost blind. They grow to about 15 cm long. Although they share the same name with snipe eels, they belong to a different family.

Long lightweights
Snipe eels may have a body that is 2 metres long, but they will only weigh 500 grammes at most.

SNIPE EEL
NEMICHTHYIDAE

DEPTH
90 m

1800 m

SIZE • UP TO 2 M

EELS

Eels are long, slender fish. There are about 740 different types of eel and they all have many backbones – vertebrae – in their long, bendy bodies. Most eels have a smooth or slimy skin, without any scales and they feed on other animals.

Conger eels will eat a range of prey, including crabs, fish and worms.

CONGER EEL

Conger eels can grow huge and powerful. They have been known to attack divers, and can deliver a nasty bite. They are the longest type of eel and can grow to 3 metres in length.

The stripes make the banded snake eel look like a venomous sea snake.

BANDED SNAKE EEL

Banded snake eels hunt at night, and find their prey using their good sense of smell. They feed on fish and crustaceans.

Slimy skin
Moray eels can make a toxic slime that coats their skin.

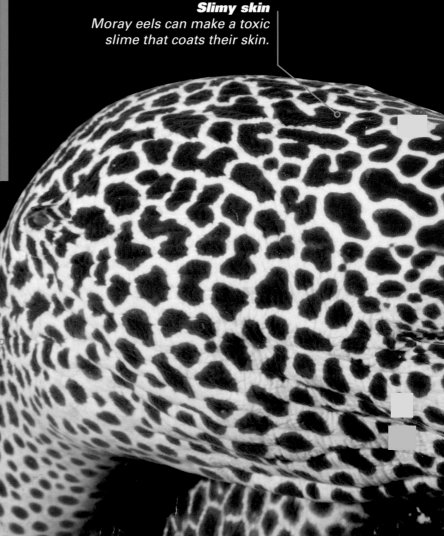

Bold patterns
This moray is called a leopard moray because of the patterns on its skin.

Ribbon eels grow up to 1 metre long and can live for 20 years.

RIBBON EEL

Ribbon eels are small moray eels. They hide under rocks or in sand, and come out to catch small fish or shrimps that swim by.

MORAY EEL

Moray eels often hide in a shallow sea's shadows. They wait for fish, or other animals to swim by, then pounce on them. Some moray eels can be more than 3 m long.

GARDEN EELS

Garden eels hide in burrows in the seabed and poke their heads out to feed. They tend to live in groups and look like plants growing in a garden.

Strong jaws
The mouth is lined with large sharp teeth.

LIVING IN GROUPS

There is safety in numbers in the deep ocean. Animals that live on land have plenty of places to keep out of sight, but in the huge expanse of the ocean there are few places to hide. Instead, animals often stay together in big groups.

Shoal
A large group of fish is called a school, or a shoal.

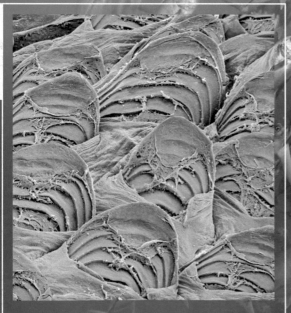

FISH SCALES
Fish scales overlap, like roof tiles, so water can flow over them easily. They are also flat, which helps to reflect light.

A shoal of hammerhead sharks swimming near the Galápagos Islands.

HAMMERHEAD SHARKS
Most sharks live alone, but hammerheads are unusual because they often live together. They split up when it is time to eat, and hunt alone.

Big-eye trevallies
These fish can grow to more than 120 centimetres long.

Silvery scales
Scales can work like mirrors, to reflect light.

About 8,000 species of fish live on coral reefs around the world.

BIGEYE TREVALLIES

When a big, swirling ball of fish is on the move the light dances off their silvery scales, and makes them look like one large animal. These reflections also confuse any predators.

CORAL REEF SHOAL

Groups of fish are common around a coral reef. There is enough food for them all to eat, and finding a mate is easier when you live together. There are plenty of eyes looking out for predators and plenty of places to hide.

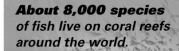

Barracuda can swim at speeds of more than 40 km/h to catch prey

SHOAL OF BARRACUDA

Barracudas have long, sleek bodies and can grow to 2 metres long. Adults usually swim alone, but young ones gather in large shoals.

DRAGONFISH

With bristling teeth, flashing lights, and a feeler dangling from its chin, the dragonfish is a monster of the deep. The females are larger than males and live for several breeding seasons. Males live only a few weeks.

Lighting up
Dragonfish make their own light through chemical reactions inside their bodies.

BLACK DRAGONFISH
IDIACANTHUS FASCIOLA

DEPTH

500 m

1800 m

SIZE • 30–40 CM
(female)

Big teeth
Sloane's viperfish has the largest teeth of any fish, relative to the size of its head.

IN THE FAMILY
Other monstrous relations of the black dragonfish also have light organs and sharp teeth. They include loosejaws and viperfish.

COLOURS

Unlike most other bioluminescent fish, the dragonfish can produce different colours from its photophores.

The barbel is tipped with a luminescent organ.

Light organ
A female has a light organ behind each eye and rows of small lights along her sides.

FEARSOME FEMALES

The female dragonfish has a long, black, streamlined body and a huge mouth with sharp teeth. Males are smaller, pale brown, and have no teeth or barbels.

Sharp teeth
Females' teeth are long, barbed fangs.

Barbel
A female also has a long feeler called a barbel.

Small head
Compared to its body, the female's head is small and dominated by its wide jaw.

Dragonfish larva

GROWING UP

Dragonfish young hatch from eggs. Before becoming adults, they grow into transparent larvae whose eyes stick out from the sides of their bodies on long stalks.

FACT FILE

DIET
Females eat small fish, but males do not feed once they are fully grown

HABITAT
Depths of the ocean, surface when feeding

DEEP-SEA FISH

Far below the sunlit surface lies a zone of darkness inhabited by some strange fish. This area has some light, as many fish create their own through bioluminescence. Most food drifts down to the depths from the surface, but some creatures do hunt.

Long, thin fish
Gulper eels will grow to about 1 metre in length.

Unusual fish
The body has no scales, pelvic fins, or swim bladder.

Giant mouth
Lined with teeth. the mouth acts like a net, opening and ambushing prey much larger that itself.

Big mouth
The gulper eel is also called the pelican eel because its mouth looks like that of the big-throated bird.

GULPER EEL

A gulper eel's long, thin body is not ideal for swimming fast. Instead, it uses the luminescent organ on its tail to attract prey. Gulper eels have been found living at depths of up to 3000 metres.

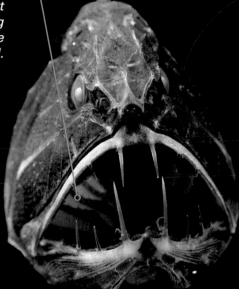

Barrier
The teeth prevent prey from escaping before they are swallowed.

 # LIGHT ORGANS

Unlike anglerfish, the light organ of the gulper eel is found at the end of the tail. In order to lure prey near its mouth, the eel has to pull the tip of its tail round towards its head.

Huge stomach
This fish's stomach has stretched to fit in a fish.

SABERTOOTH FISH

This small fierce-looking predator has tubular eyes that point upwards and large pointed front teeth, which give it its name.

BLACK SWALLOWER

This fish can also swallow prey much larger than itself. It inhabits depths of 2,745 m and feeds on bony fish, which are swallowed whole into its enormous, stretchy stomach.

OARFISH

Oarfish are the longest bony fish in the world, growing up to 11 metres long. Although they sometimes hunt at depths of 1000 metres, oarfish sometimes swim near the surface, and may get washed ashore.

Terrifying tail
The whip-like tail glows pink at the end and also helps the eel to move.

Sea monster
These strange fish may be to blame for stories of giant sea serpents!

MICROLIFE

The oceans are home to billions of tiny animals and plants. They are too small for us to see and we can only look at them with the help of a microscope. They are called microlife, or plankton, and other animals depend on them for food.

MICROLIFE

DEPTH

0 m

100 m

SIZE • UP TO 1 CM

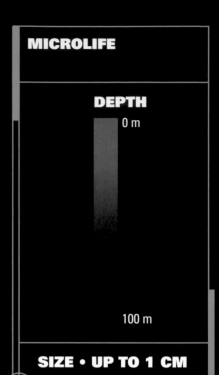

Tail
Tiny animals use thread-like tails to swim.

PHYTOPLANKTON BLOOM

When conditions are just right, tiny plant plankton can grow into huge swarms, called a bloom. Some blooms, like this one in the Bay of Biscay, can be seen from space.

0   100 km   200 km   300 km

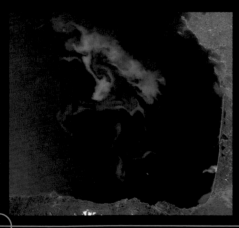

Copepod
These animals have two long antennae. They are members of the crustacean family.

This microscope image of plant plankton has been enlarged 20 times.

Plant plankton

PLANT PLANKTON

Plant plankton, or phytoplankton, is made up of tiny plants that use the sun's energy to make food. They make the oxygen we breathe.

ANIMALS

Animal plankton
is known as
zooplankton.
The name comes
from the Greek
meaning 'animal
wanderer'.

Float along
*Some plankton
can swim, but
they mostly
float in the
ocean.*

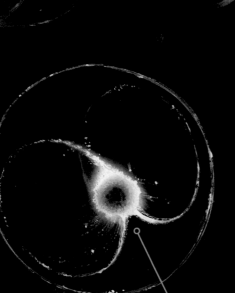

Ocean young
*Some tiny animals are the eggs
and young of fish, jellyfish and
other sea creatures.*

 MICRO ZOO

Animals and plants that are too small for us to
see are described as microscopic. Larger
plankton feed on smaller plankton, and they are
eaten by fish, which are eaten by even bigger
fish, and so on. Without these tiny living things,
nothing else would live in the oceans.

DIET
Tiny plants

HABITAT
*All the world's oceans, near
the surface*

TINY CREATURES

Small animals and plants are the food for bigger animals in the sea. While some of these creatures have simple bodies and lives, others are the young of bigger animals, such as octopuses, that have just hatched. Young sea animals are often called larvae.

Soft skin
The octopus's soft skin is coloured and patterned.

WATER FLEA

Water fleas are transparent, so it is possible to see their body parts inside. They use their antennae to swim around.

Tiny version
An octopus larva looks like the adult, but it is much smaller.

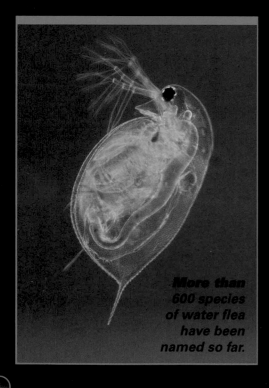

More than 600 species of water flea have been named so far.

 ## PACIFIC GIANT OCTOPUS LARVA

A giant Pacific octopus is one of the biggest animals in the ocean, but its larvae (young) measure about 1 cm when they hatch from their eggs.

STARFISH LARVA

A female starfish lays millions of eggs. Each larva grows 'arms' out from its body and it takes two months to become an adult.

Arm with tiny suckers

HEART URCHIN LARVA

A sea urchin larva floats in the water for several weeks before it settles on the seabed and grows into an adult. It has several arms that stretch out around the mouth.

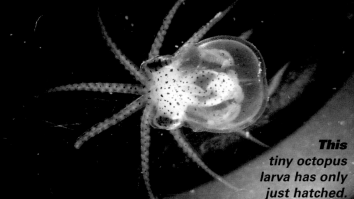

This tiny octopus larva has only just hatched.

HUGE NUMBERS

Octopus eggs are produced in huge numbers – about 45,000 each time. The larvae hatch and grow quickly, although very few of them will survive to maturity.

JAPANESE SPIDER CRAB

Japanese spider crabs are the largest crabs in the world and they can measure 4 metres from toe to toe – about as wide as a car. These giant crustaceans stay on the seabed, searching for food to eat.

Long legs
The crab's body does not get much bigger as it ages, but its legs get longer.

SPIDER CRAB
MACROCHEIRA KAEMPFERI

DEPTH
50 m

600 m

SIZE • UP TO 4 M

FACT FILE

DIET
Small animals, dead animals, seaweed

HABITAT
The sandy or rocky seabed of coastal areas

SMALL MOUTHS
Japanese spider crabs tear up food into small pieces with their pincers before putting it in their mouths.

The body of a spider crab is only about 40 cm across.

Spines
Spines grow
between the eyes.

Scavengers
Japanese spider crabs
feed off the remains
of dead sea creatures
and anything else
they can find.

Carapace
A crab's tough shell is
called a carapace. It is
red, tan or orange with
blotches of white.

**Indonesian
spider crab**

*Indonesian spider crabs sometimes
cover their bodies with stinging hydrozoa.*

WEAK LEGS

The legs of a
Japanese sea crab
are spindly. The
weight of its body is
supported by water
so the legs do not
need to be strong.
However, this also
means that they are
easily snapped.
Luckily, the crabs can
grow new legs to
replace ones that
they lose!

CAMOUFLAGE

Some types of spider crab, such as
the Indonesian spider crab, are
called 'decorators' because they
cover their bodies with bits of
seaweed or small animals.

OCEAN ARTHROPODS

It is thought that about three-quarters of all types of animals are arthropods, including insects. Arthropods have a tough outer skin, a body that is divided into segments, and jointed legs. Crabs, prawns, lobsters and sea spiders are all types of arthropod.

HORSESHOE CRAB

Horseshoe crabs are living fossils. They are the last members of a family of arthropods that lived 300 million years ago. They are more closely related to spiders than to crabs. They walk about the ocean floor looking for worms and molluscs to eat.

Green, paddle-shaped antenna

The peacock mantis has the fastest punch of any living animal.

SEA SPIDER

Despite their name, sea spiders are not really spiders! They have between 8 and twelve legs, and feed on corals and sponges.

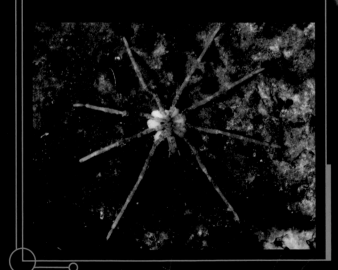

PEACOCK MANTIS

Peacock mantises are among the most colourful of all sea creatures. They are shrimps with incredible eyesight, and a powerful punch.

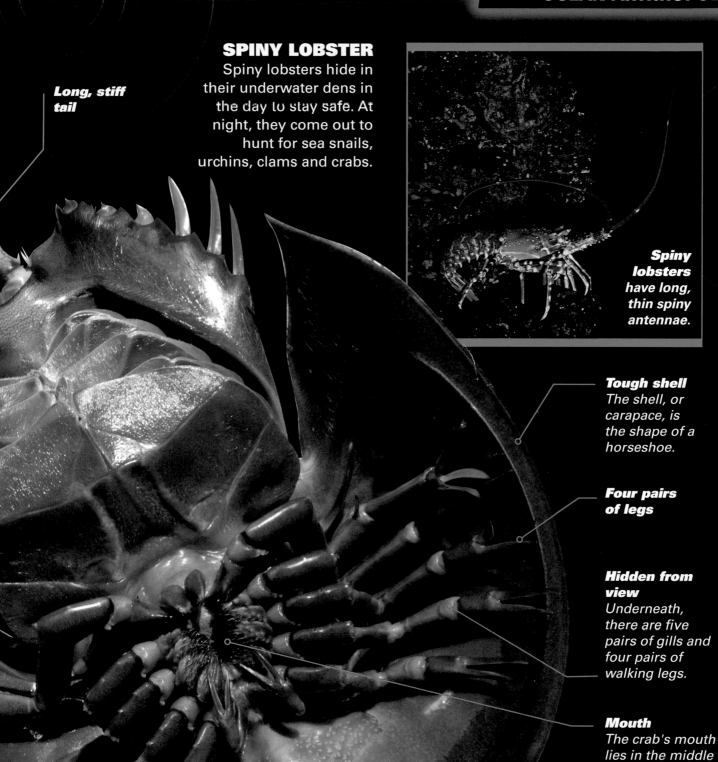

SPINY LOBSTER
Spiny lobsters hide in their underwater dens in the day to stay safe. At night, they come out to hunt for sea snails, urchins, clams and crabs.

Long, stiff tail

Spiny lobsters have long, thin spiny antennae.

Tough shell
The shell, or carapace, is the shape of a horseshoe.

Four pairs of legs

Hidden from view
Underneath, there are five pairs of gills and four pairs of walking legs.

Mouth
The crab's mouth lies in the middle of its legs.

Front side
Small caption to add if necessary.

FIREFLY SQUID

Light organs
Two of the arms contain light-emitting organs.

Arms
Like all squid, the firefly squid has eight arms.

In spring, millions of tiny firefly squid come to the surface to breed. They produce glittering lights to frighten or confuse predators and also to attract mates. However, in Japan firefly squid are a delicacy and the lights attract fishermen as well.

JAPANESE FIREFLY SQUID
WATASENIA SCINTILLANS

DEPTH

200 m

400 m

SIZE • UP TO 7 CM

FIREFLY SQUID

The firefly squid's body and tentacles contain small light organs, which produce blue-white lights. The squid can alter the colour, intensity, and angle of its lights.

SMALL BUT SPEEDY
Japanese firefly squid are only the length of the human finger but they can swim up to 40 km/h.

ACTUAL SIZE

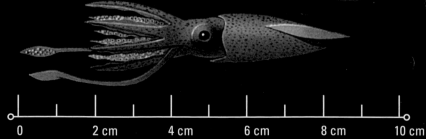

0		2 cm		4 cm		6 cm		8 cm		10 cm

DEADLY LURE

As well being used to attract a mate, the firefly squid uses its light display to lure prey. Once it is close enough, the squid will grab the prey with its arms and pull it towards the squid's mouth.

FACT FILE

DIET
Shrimp, crabs, fish, and plankton

HABITAT
Depths of the ocean, surface when feeding

Impressive eyes
A firefly squid has three types of light-sensitive cells in its retina.

Glowing lights
The body is covered with rows of glowing lights.

DEEP-SEA SQUID

The deep-sea squid produces so much light that it would show up on a photograph taken in the dark, without a flash.

Tentacles
The largest light-producing organs are found in the tentacles.

OCEAN MOLLUSCS

There are more than 50,000 types, or species, of mollusc in the world and most of them live in the oceans. Many molluscs have shells and live near the seabed, but octopuses and squid are smart, soft-bodied swimmers of the open sea.

Shell
The nautilus's soft body is protected by a hard shell.

Eye
Even though it has a large eye, a nautilus has poor vision and relies more on smell.

NUDIBRANCH

Nudibranchs, or sea slugs, are some of the most colourful of all ocean creatures. Their colours and patterns warn predators that their flesh tastes bad or is poisonous.

CONE SHELL

Many molluscs are protected by shells, but cone shells have an extra way to stay safe – they are one of the most venomous animals on the planet. Inside the shell, the animal has a spear-like barb that is fired at a fish and injects deadly venom.

Some cone shells produce a venom that is deadly to humans.

Head
*There are up
to 90 tentacles
surrounding
the head.*

NAUTILUS

These molluscs live in the warm waters around Asia and Australia. They use their tentacles to catch prey, such as shrimps. They move around by sucking in water and then forcing it out to create a high-pressure jet to push them along.

Changing skin
*The skin colour
can change all
the time, even
when the
cuttlefish is
resting.*

CUTTLEFISH

Cuttlefish can change the colour of their skin in an instant. They often live on coral reefs.

GIANT OCTOPUS

A giant octopus can grow to about 3 m long, and can live in deep water up to 750 m. These enormous predators crawl on the seafloor, or swim.

Head

LIVING FOSSILS

Nautilus are often called living fossils, because they are the last example of a group of animals called nautiloids, which evolved nearly 500 million years ago.

COMB JELLY

Comb jellies are soft-bodied animals that swim gracefully through the sea. They prey on other animals, especially young fish, which they catch using sticky tentacles that they trail through the water. As they move, they shimmer with beautiful colours.

FACT FILE

DIET
Plankton and young fish

HABITAT
Open ocean and coasts, especially warm waters

Glowing lights
Comb jellies have rows of light-producing cells along their bodies, which they flash to startle predators.

SEE-THROUGH GUTS

This comb jelly has swallowed a krill – a shrimp-like animal – which can be seen inside the jelly's gut.

SHAPES AND SIZES

There are about 200 different types of comb jelly. They come in various shapes and sizes and many have long trailing arms, which they use to catch prey.

GLOWING LIGHTS

The beautiful colours of a comb jelly can be seen as it moves. Some comb jellies produce lights by mixing chemicals, while others glow because they have eaten other bioluminescent creatures.

⊕ SWIMMING HAIRS

The body of a comb jelly is covered in rows of tiny moving 'hairs'. When the hairs beat together, the comb jelly moves forwards. As the hairs beat, they release glowing particles, creating a luminous cloud behind the comb jelly.

COMB JELLY
CTENOPHORA

DEPTH

0 m

7000 m

SIZE • UP TO 1.5 M

Soft bodies
The body is soft, with no bones or shells to protect it.

0   10 cm   20 cm   30 cm

OCEAN INVERTEBRATES

Animals that do not have backbones are called invertebrates. Many of the ocean's animals are invertebrates. Although they do not have a skeleton to support their organs and limbs, they can grow big because the water supports their weight.

BLUE SEA SQUIRT
Sea squirts look like blobs of jelly on the seabed, but they are busy little animals that suck in seawater, and eat any animals that come with it.

CORAL
A blue starfish rests on a coral. The coral is rocky, but it has been built by small invertebrates. Tiny polyps live inside the coral and build it.

Stinging tentacles

SEA ANEMONE
Sea anemones rest on the seabed. Their stinging tentacles capture animals that float or swim past.

JELLYFISH

A black sea nettle is a type of giant jellyfish. These invertebrates can grow huge, and their tentacles can reach 7 metres long or more.

Bell
This is the jellyfish's body. It can grow to 1 metre in width.

Long tentacles
They are covered with stinging cells that stun or kill their prey.

SPONGE

Red sea sponges look like plants, but they are animals that suck water into their bodies to feed on the little animals in the water. Sea sponges are stuck to the seabed.

Powerful sting
A sea nettle's sting will kill small sea creatures, but is not lethal to humans.

STINGING CELLS

The thousands of stinging cells that cover the sea nettle's tentacles are called nematocysts. These release a venom-covered dart when touched.

STARFISH

Starfish have tough bodies that are usually covered in spines, and they use their arms to creep along the seabed. They eat other animals by pushing their stomachs out of their mouths to start digesting their food straight away!

Spiny arms
Most starfish have five arms, but some have more.

LARVA STAGE
Starfish release many eggs into the sea. They hatch into larvae that float in the plankton. Eventually, they settle and grow into adults.

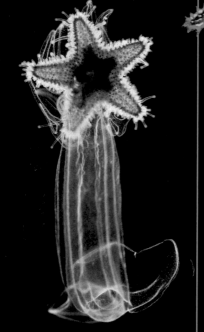

The larval stage of a starfish.

Tough shell
The shell of a starfish is made of lots of small pieces, or 'plates'.

CROWN OF THORNS STARFISH
Crown of thorns starfish devour coral polyps in a coral reef, causing terrible damage to these precious places.

A crown of thorns starfish crawls over a coral reef.

ECHINODERMS

Brittle stars and starfish belong to an animal group called the echinoderms. They do not have heads. Brittlestars raise their arms into the water and use them to catch prey.

Brittle star
Brittle stars are not starfish, but they are similar.

Spines
The spines catch animals in the water that flows past the star.

Arms and body
A brittle star uses its arms to feed and to walk. The disc in the centre is its body.

FACT FILE

DIET
Fish, sea urchins, other starfish

HABITAT
Coral reefs and coastal waters

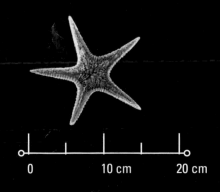

0   10 cm   20 cm

STARFISH
ASTEROIDEA

DEPTH

0 m

6000 m

SIZE • UP TO 15 CM

ON THE OCEAN FLOOR

Near to land, the oceans are shallow and sunlight and warmth can reach the sea floor. The seabed here makes a good home for many animals. Farther out to sea, there is less light and the seafloor can be a dark, empty and almost lifeless place.

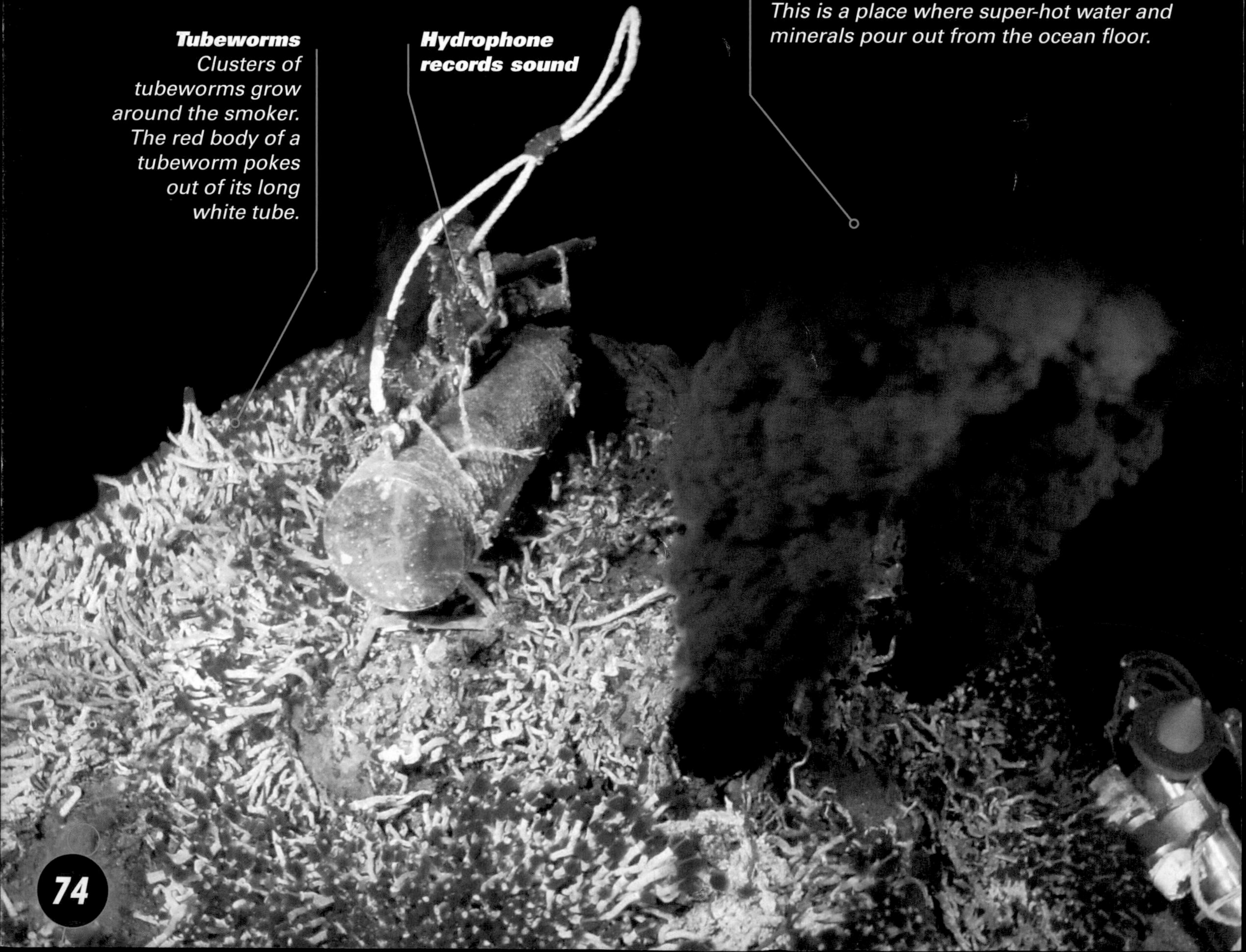

GIANT TUBEWORM
RIFTIA PACHYPTILA

DEPTH
1,600 m

6000 m

SIZE • UP TO 2.5 M

Smoker
This is a place where super-hot water and minerals pour out from the ocean floor.

Tubeworms
Clusters of tubeworms grow around the smoker. The red body of a tubeworm pokes out of its long white tube.

Hydrophone records sound

SEA CUCUMBER

Sea cucumbers swallow mud and sand, and feed on bits of dead animals or plants within it. Some sea cucumbers graze on seaweed.

A red-lined sea cucumber crawling over the Great Barrier Reef.

Juvenile fish hide among the spines of this radiant sea urchin.

SEA URCHINS

The long spines of a sea urchin can deliver a painful dose of venom. These prickly animals mostly live in warm coastal places.

SEA SMOKERS

There are places on the seabed where hot water and minerals escape under the seabed. Strange animals, such as tubeworms, live here and feed on the minerals.

Probe measures levels of hydrogen

CHRISTMAS TREE WORM

Christmas tree worms are named after their beautiful spiral of colourful tentacles. They feed on plankton that they take out of the water.

FEATHER STAR

Feather stars are also called sea lilies and they are a type of echinoderm, not a plant. Long feathery arms surround the feather star's mouth and are held up, into the water. These arms, or tentacles, capture plankton in the water and move it towards the animal's mouth.

GLOSSARY

APHOTIC ZONE
The part of the ocean beneath the Photic Zone, which stretches down to a depth of about 200 metres. No light reaches down to the Aphotic Zone.

BALEEN
Plates made of keratin inside the mouths of whales such as humpback whales and blue whales. The whales use the baleen plates to filter small fish and krill from the water.

BLOWHOLE
A hole at the top of the heads of whales and dolphins. The animals only breathe through their blowholes, not through their mouths.

BONY FISH
Fish whose skeleton is made from bone rather than from cartilage.

BREACHING
When an animal leaps out of the water completely. Some sharks breach to catch prey, while scientists are unsure why some whales and dolphins breach. They may be trying to get rid of parasites or just showing off.

CARAPACE
The tough upper shell found on crabs, turtles, spiders and other arachnids.

CARTILAGE
A flexible substance found in some of our joints and in our ears and noses. A shark's whole skeleton is made of cartilage.

FINS
Flaps on the sides of sea creatures such as fish and whales, which they use to swim.

FISH
Animals that live in water and breathe using gills. Fish use muscles attached to their backbones and fins to move their bodies in an 'S' shape.

FLIPPERS
Limbs of some sea-going animals that are used for swimming. In penguins, the wings have adapted to become flippers. In turtles and seals, the flippers are their modified arms and legs.

FLUKES
The horizontal parts of a whale's tail. They are moved up and down to push the whale through the water.

GILL
A body part in fish and some amphibians that allows them to breathe underwater. The gills take in oxygen that is dissolved in the water.

HATCHLING
The name given to a young reptile or bird that has just hatched out of its shell.

INVERTEBRATE
An animal that does not have a backbone. Most animals are invertebrates. Some of these have a hard outer exoskeleton, while others have bodies that are completely soft.

KRILL

Small shrimp-like creatures that are found in large numbers in the oceans. Krill are the main food of many fish, squid and whales.

LARVAE

The young of animals such as fish, insects and amphibians. The larvae often look completely different from the adults, and can live in very different parts of the ocean.

LURE

The long, thin fin found on the heads of anglerfish. A lure is used attract a prey.

MIGRATION

Going on a long journey in search of food or a good place to breed and raise young.

PHOTIC ZONE

The uppermost part of the ocean, down to a depth of about 200 metres, where light can reach.

PHOTOPHORE

The light-making organs found on some fish and other creatures that glow in the dark.

PLANKTON

The name given to tiny microscopic living things found in the ocean. There are two types of plankton – phytoplankton, which is made up of miniature plants, and zooplankton, which consists of tiny animals.

POD

The name given to a group of whales or dolphins.

REPTILE

A group of animals that have scaly skin and lay eggs. Reptiles are cold-blooded, which means they cannot keep their body temperature constant. Crocodiles, turtles and lizards are all reptiles.

SCALES

Small protective plates that form part of the outer skin of some animals. Fish have bony scales, while reptiles and birds have scales made of keratin.

SPECIES

A kind of living thing. Members of the same species are very similar to one another and can breed and produce offspring.

SPERMACETI

A waxy substance found in the heads of whales. It may help a whale to float and it may also be used to produce sounds.

SPY HOPPING

The habit of poking a head above the water's surface to look for prey or predators. Spy hopping is performed by whales and some sharks.

SUBMERSIBLE

A miniature submarine designed to dive down to extreme depths. Submersibles can be robotic or they can carry people.

TUSK

An enlarged tooth that sticks out of an animal's mouth. Narwhals and walruses have tusks.

VENOM

A toxic substance that can cause a painful wound, or in the worst cases, paralysis and even death.

INDEX

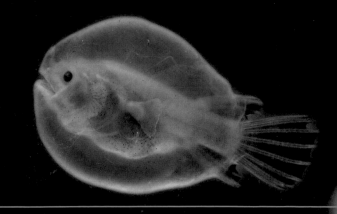

ACKNOWLEDGEMENT'S

Picture credits

(t=top, b=bottom, l=left, r=right, c=centre, fc=front cover)

123RF: Andreas Altenburger 59 bc

Corbis: © Dave Fleetham/Design Pics/Corbis 14 bl

FLPA: Frans Lanting/FLPA 9 tc, Hiroya Minakuchi/Minden Pictures/FLPA 9 br, 11 cr, 14 l, 29 r, 37 br, Fabien Michenet/Biosphoto/ FLPA 10-11 c, Tui De Roy/Minden Pictures/FLPA 10 bl, Norbert Wu/Minden Pictures/FLPA 14-15 c, 17 cl, 26 tcl, 30 bl, 31 tr, 34 tr, 37 tr, 45 br, 55 br, 69 tr, 75 c, Chris & Tilde Stuart/FLPA 13 bc, 15 cr, Roger Tidman/FLPA 11 bc, 17 bc, Brandon Cole/Biosphoto/ FLPA 15 br, 37 bcr, Samuel Blanc/Biosphoto/FLPA 17 tc, Mark Sisson/FLPA 19 tc, Chris Stenger/Minden Pictures/FLPA 19 br, SA Team/FN/Minden/FLPA 20 tcl, Peter Reynolds/FLPA 20 bl, Reinhard Dirscherl/FLPA 22-23 c, 36 cl, 48-49 c, 51 cr, 66-67 c, Photo Researchers/FLPA 23 cl, 47 tc, 58-59 c, Flip Nicklin/Minden Pictures/FLPA 25 cl, 36 bl, Mike Parry/Minden Pictures/FLPA 25 br, Patricio Robles Gil/Minden Pictures/FLPA 28 c, Mathieu Pujol/Biosphoto/FLPA 29 bl, Imagebroker/FLPA 28 bl, 33 tr, 36 bcl, OceanPhoto/FLPA 33 br, Richard Herrmann/Minden Pictures/FLPA 36-37 c, 70-71 c, Fred Bavendam/Minden Pictures/FLPA 32 bl, 49 tr, 67 br, 75 br, IMAGEBROKER, NORBERT PROBST/Imagebroker/FLPA 32 bcl, 50-51 c, 72 bcl, 75 tr, 75 cr, Peter David/FLPA 46 c, D P Wilson/FLPA 48 tcl, 56 bc, 59 tr, 59 cr, Norbert Probst/Imagebroker/FLPA 49 tcr, Chris Newbert/Minden Pictures/FLPA 50 bcl, Colin Marshall/FLPA 51 bl, 70 cl, H. Eisenbeiss/FLPA 58 bl, Birgitte Wilms/Minden Pictures/FLPA 61 cr, Albert Lleal/ Minden Pictures/FLPA 27 r, 63 br, Manfred Bail/Imagebroker/FLPA 62 bl, Steve Trewhella/FLPA 62 br, Gerard Lacz/FLPA 63 tr, Colin Marshall/FLPA 66 cl, 67 cr, 70 cl, 70 bl, IMAGEBROKER, MICHAEL MOXTER/Imagebroker/FLPA 71 br

Getty: Gavin Parsons 18-19 c, Lisa Graham 18 bl, Brian J. Skerry 18 bc, Mauricio Handler 20 cl, Wolfgang Poelzer 22 bl, 27 tcr, Tobias Bernhard 22 cl, David Jenkins 24 cl, Jones/Shimlock-Secret Sea Visions 26-27 c

Naturepl: © DOC WHITE/naturepl.com 13 cr, © David Shale/naturepl.com 43 tr, © David Shale/naturepl.com 47 cr, © Visuals Unlimited/naturepl.com 60-61 c, © Solvin Zankl/naturepl.com 42 cl, © Jurgen Freund/naturepl.com 48 cl, © Franco Banfi/naturepl.com 30 br

Shutterstock: OlegD 62-63 c

SPL: Jeff Rotman/SCIENCE PHOTO LIBRARY 6 cl, ALEXIS ROSENFELD/SCIENCE PHOTO LIBRARY 6 bc, DAVID FLEETHAM, VISUALS UNLIMITED /SCIENCE PHOTO LIBRARY 66 bl, NOAA PMEL Vents Program/SCIENCE PHOTO LIBRARY 74 bl, SUSUMU NISHINAGA/SCIENCE PHOTO LIBRARY 50 bl

Superstock: Reinhard Dirscherl/age fotostock/SuperStock 13 tcl, age fotostock/SuperStock 28-29 c, 35 bc, Norbert Probst/imagebroker/imagebroker.net/SuperStock 32-33 c, Stuart Westmorland/Science Faction/SuperStock 35 tr, 42 bl, BlueGreen Pictures/SuperStock 53 tr, Minden Pictures/SuperStock 72 lc